# Plastic

## Chris Oxlade

Heinemann
LIBRARY

**www.heinemann.co.uk/library**
Visit our website to find out more information about **Heinemann Library** books.

To Order:
    Phone 44 (0) 1865 888066
    Send a fax to 44 (0) 1865 314091
    Visit the Heinemann Library Bookshop at www.heinemann.co.uk/library to browse
    our catalogue and order online.

First published in Great Britain by Heinemann Library, Halley Court, Jordan Hill, Oxford OX2 8EJ
a division of Reed Educational and Professional Publishing Ltd.
Heinemann is a registered trademark of Reed Educational & Professional Publishing Ltd.

OXFORD  MELBOURNE  AUCKLAND  JOHANNESBURG  BLANTYRE
GABORONE IBADAN PORTSMOUTH (NH) USA  CHICAGO

Designed by Storeybooks
Originated by Ambassador Litho Ltd.
Printed in Hong Kong / China

ISBN 0 431 12721 2 (hardback)    ISBN 0 431 12728 X (paperback)
05 04 03 02    06 05 04 03 02
10 9 8 7 6 5 4 3 2    10 9 8 7 6 5 4 3 2 1

**British Library Cataloguing in Publication Data**
    Oxlade, Chris
    Plastic. – (Materials)
    1. Plastic
    I. Title
    620.1'923

**Acknowledgements**
Barnaby's Picture Library /H. K. Maitland p.19; Corbis pp.24, /Bob Krist p.4, Image Bank p.11; Kate
Bryant-Mole p.16; Noel Whittal p.29; Oxford Scientific Films/Edward Parker p.26; Photodisc p.14; PPL
Library p.15; Science Photo Library p. 27; Shell Library pp.17, 22; Stone p.12; Tudor Photography pp.5, 6,
7, 8, 9, 10, 13, 18, 20, 23, 25.

Cover photograph reproduced with permission of Tudor Photography.

Every effort has been made to contact copyright holders of any material reproduced in this book.
Any omissions will be rectified in subsequent printings if notice is given to the Publisher.

# Contents

You can find words shown in bold, **like this** in the Glossary.

# What is plastic?

Plastic is a man-made material. It is made in factories from **chemicals**. These plastic beads have just been **manufactured**. They will be made into plastic things.

Plastic is an important material. People make many different things from it. All the things on this page are made from plastic. They are called plastic objects.

# Hard and soft plastics

Some plastics are very hard. They
are difficult to stretch or bend.
When hard plastics are stretched
or bent, they may snap in two.

Some plastics are very soft. They are easy to stretch or bend. When soft plastic is stretched a lot it does not go back into shape afterwards.

# Hot and cold plastics

There are two different families of plastics. The plastics in one family go soft when they are warmed up. They go hard again when they cool down. These are called thermoplastics.

The plastics in the other family do not go soft when they are warmed up. They stay hard instead. These are called thermosetting plastics.

# Waterproof plastics

All kinds of plastic are **waterproof**. They don't let water through and water does not soak into them. You can make paper or card waterproof by covering them with plastic, like this map.

Because plastics are waterproof, they last for a very long time. They don't **rot** away like wood, and they don't **rust** like **steel**, even if they are left outside.

# Electricity and heat

Plastics don't let **electricity** pass through them. They are called electrical **insulators**. Telephone wires that carry electricity are covered in plastic. This stops the electricity flowing to other wires.

This drinking cup is made from a plastic called **expanded** polystyrene. This plastic is full of tiny air bubbles. It does not let heat pass through it. It stops the heat from burning the person's hands.

# Making plastics

Plastics are made in factories from **chemicals**. Most of the chemicals come from **oil** found underground or beneath the sea. Different plastics are made by mixing different chemicals together.

Some plastics are made just before they are used. The plastic for this boat **hull** was made by mixing two liquids together. After a few minutes, the plastic became hard.

# Shaping plastics

Many plastic objects, or things, are made in a **mould**. Hot, runny plastic is poured into the mould. When the plastic has gone hard again, the new object is taken out of the mould.

Long, thin plastic objects are made by pushing hot, runny plastic through a hole. This is called extrusion. Plastic pipes and **fibres** are made like this.

# Bottles and tubes

Plastic containers are useful for storing drinks and other liquids. Plastic is often used for bottles instead of glass. Plastic bottles do not smash if they fall, and are lighter to carry than glass ones.

Plastic pipes and tubes carry liquids and gases. These strong plastic pipes are being laid underground. They carry gas for cooking and heating. They will last longer than metal pipes.

# Plastic packaging

Thin sheets of plastic are used to make shopping bags and wrapping for foods. Some plastics are wrapped around objects and then heated up to make them shrink.

**Expanded** polystyrene is a kind of plastic. It is a strong, light material often used for packaging. It is full of tiny air bubbles. It protects things from bumps and scrapes.

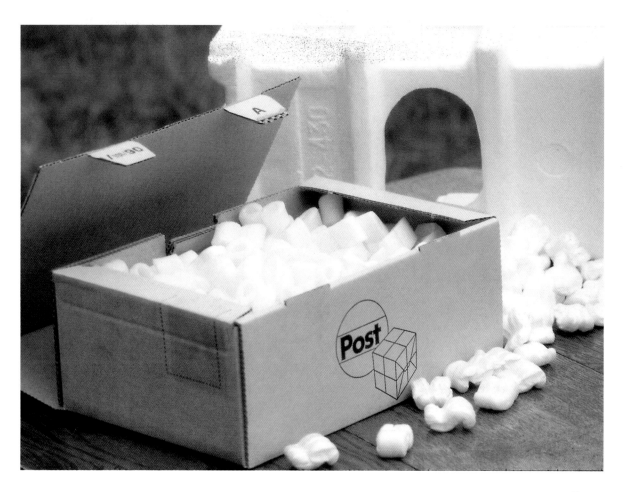

# Plastic fibres and fabrics

A **fibre** is a thin strand of material, such as a hair. Plastic fibres are made by pushing hot, runny plastic through tiny holes. These fibres are made of a plastic called nylon.

A fabric is made by joining fibres together.
Fabrics like fleece are made with plastic
fibres. They last a long time and don't
go baggy.

# Building with plastic

Builders often use plastics instead of other materials. These screens are made of hard, see-through plastic. They don't shatter if people run into them.

Window frames, doors, gutters and pipes are made from a plastic called PVC. This lasts a long time. It is strong and **waterproof**, and does not need to be painted like wood or metal.

# Recycling plastics

Plastic is a useful material because it does not **rot**, but this also causes problems. When we throw away plastic things, they last for ever. There is then too much rubbish.

Some plastic things, such as bottles, can be collected and **recycled**. They are melted down to make plastic beads and then made into new things.

# Fact file

▶ Plastic is a man-made, or synthetic, material. It is not a **natural** material. It is made in factories from **chemicals** made from **oil**.

▶ Some kinds of plastic are hard and difficult to stretch. Some kinds are soft and easy to stretch.

▶ Some kinds of plastic go soft when they are heated. Other kinds of plastic stay hard.

▶ Plastics are **waterproof**. They don't **rot** away.

▶ **Electricity** and heat do not flow through plastics.

▶ Plastics are not attracted by **magnets**.

# Would you believe it?

A plastic called kevlar is stronger than the metal **steel**, but weighs less than steel. You could hang on a kevlar **fibre** as thin as the lead inside a pencil. This person is hanging on kevlar fibres.

# Glossary

**chemicals**  special materials that are used in factories and homes to do many jobs, including cleaning and protecting

**electricity**  form of energy. We use electricity to make electric machines work.

**expanded**  made bigger

**fibre**  long, thin piece of material, like a hair

**hull**  main part of a boat or ship that sits in the water

**insulator**  material that does not let electricity or heat flow through it

**magnet**  object that attracts iron and steel

**manufactured**  made in a factory

**mould**  shape that runny plastic is poured into to make a plastic object

**natural**  comes from plants, animals or the rocks in the earth

**oil**  thick, black liquid found underground or under the sea. We get lots of useful chemicals from oil. Some are used to make plastics. Petrol for cars also comes from oil.

**recycle**  use again instead of throwing away

**rot**  go soft and crumbly. Wood rots when it gets damp. Most plastic does not rot.

**rust**  browny-red substance that forms on iron or steel when it is left out in the rain or wet

**steel**  strong, hard metal

**waterproof**  does not let water in or out

# More books to read

*My World of Science: Materials*
Angela Royston
Heinemann Library, 2001

*Science All Around Me: Materials*
Karen Bryant-Mole
Heinemann Library, 1996

*Images: Materials and Their Properties*
Big Book Compilation
Heinemann Library, 1999

*Find Out About Plastic*
Henry Pluckrose, Franklin Watts

*I Can Help Recycle Rubbish*
Franklin Watts

# Index